Seductive Patterns
Coloring Book for Adults

by Asma Zergui

ISBN-13:
978-1511963176

ISBN-10:
1511963174

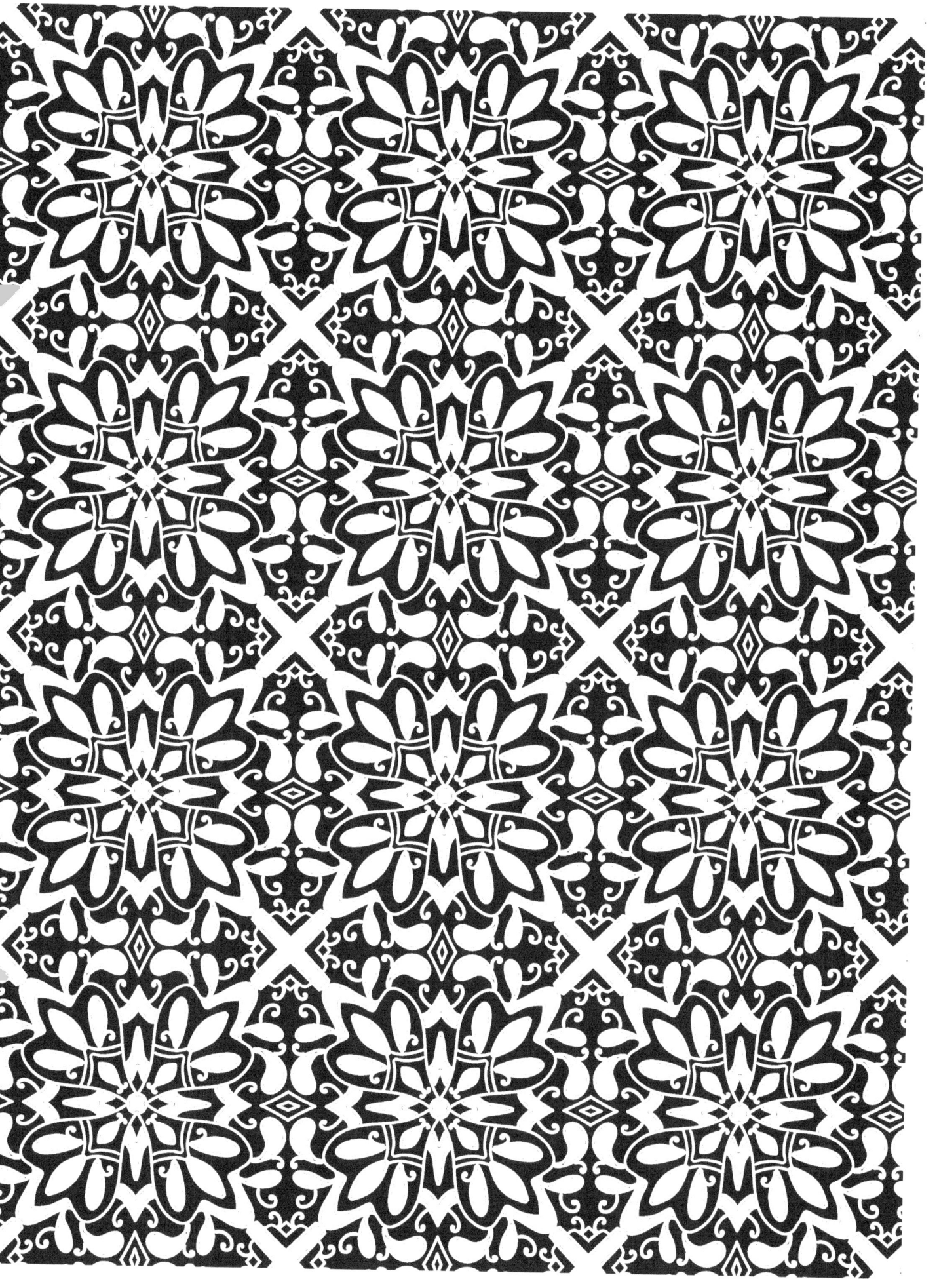

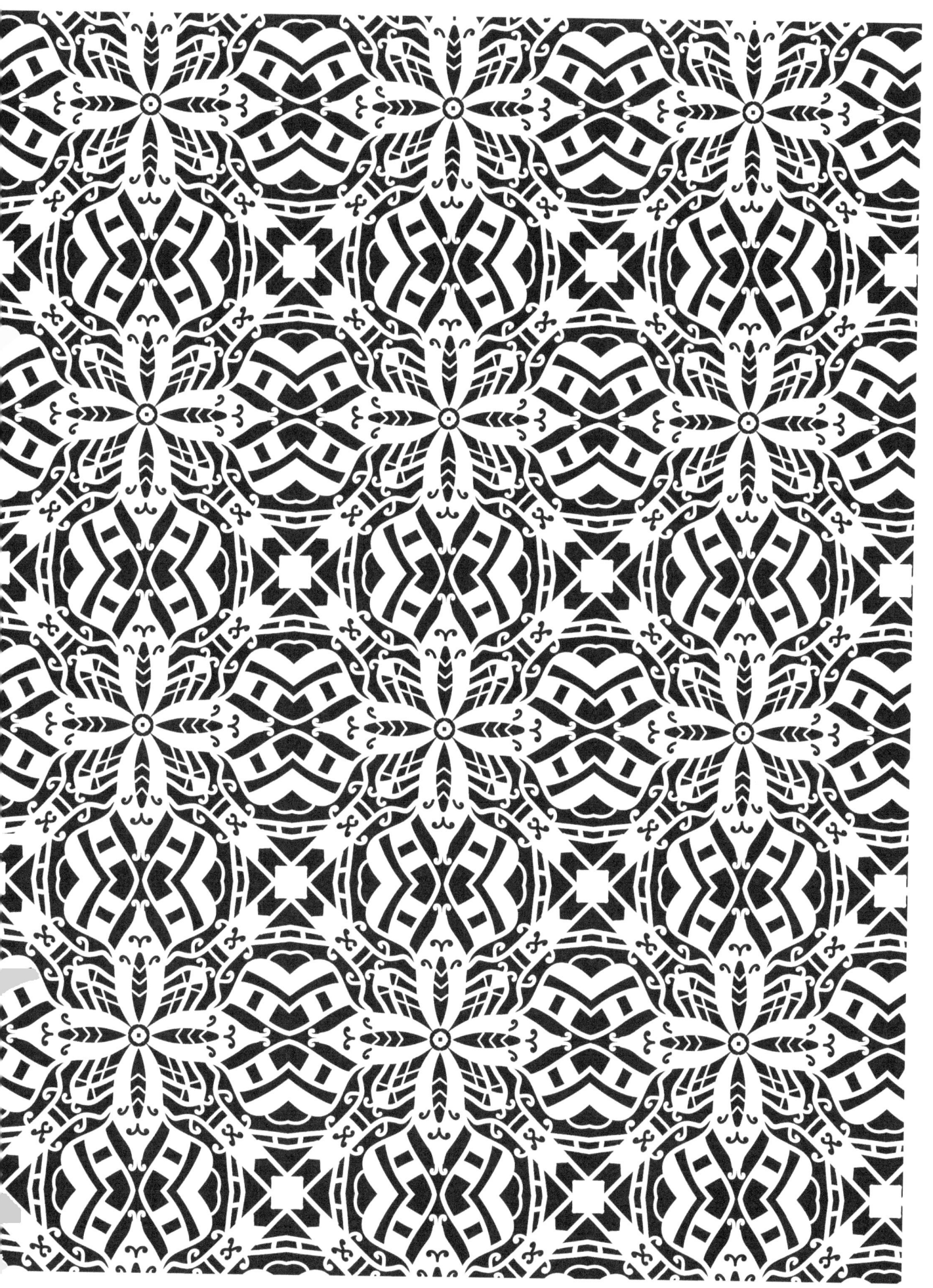

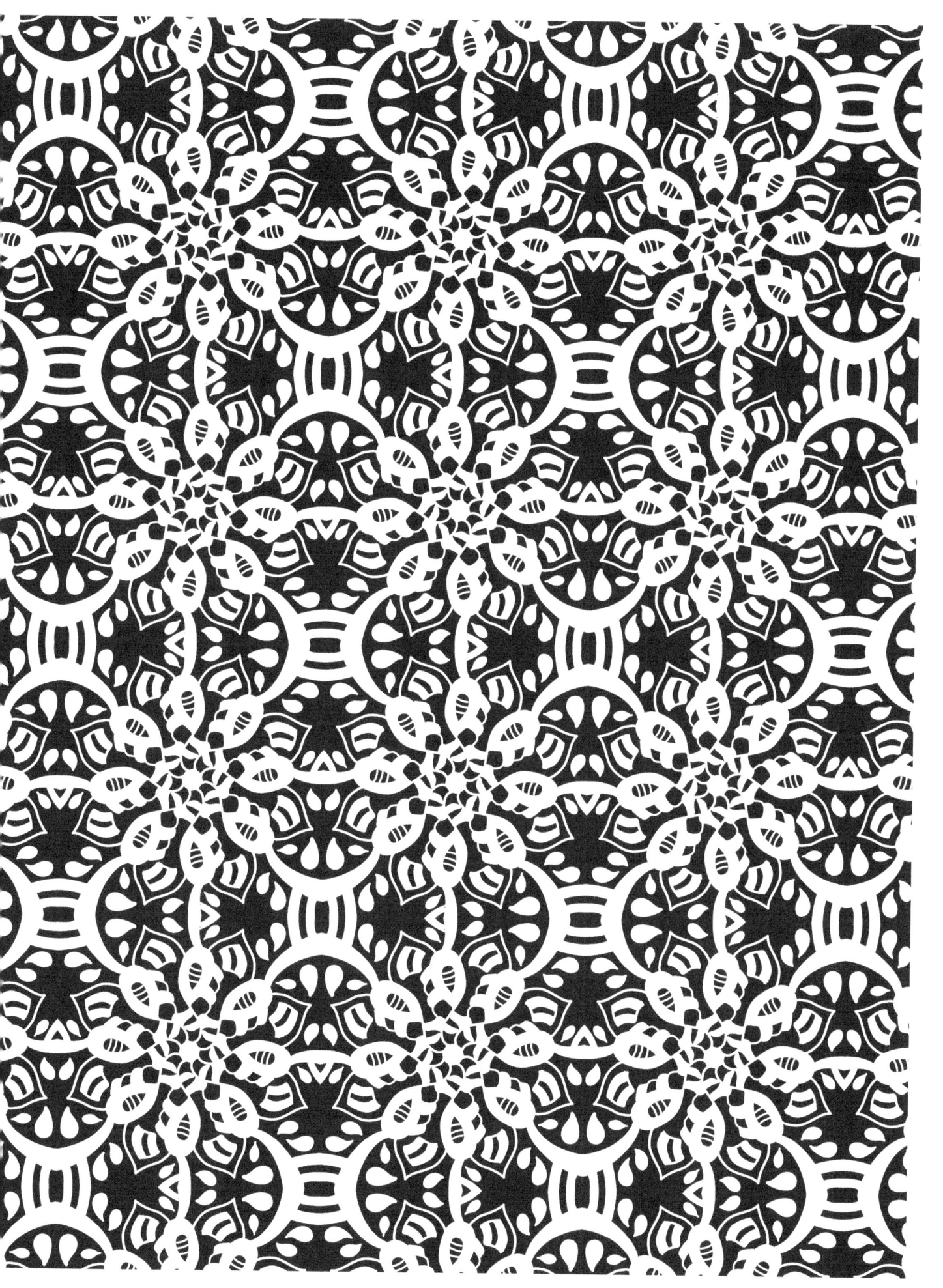

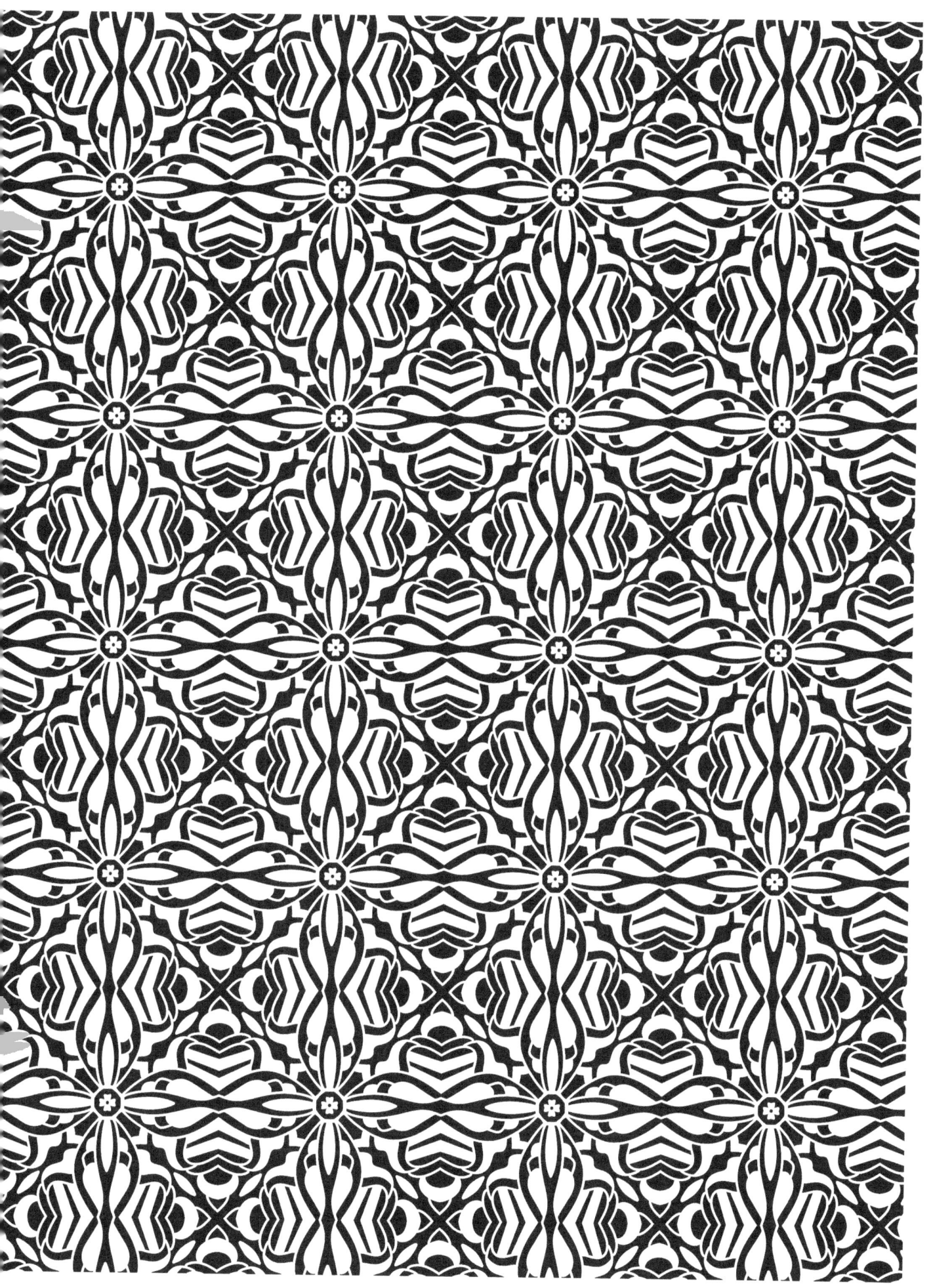

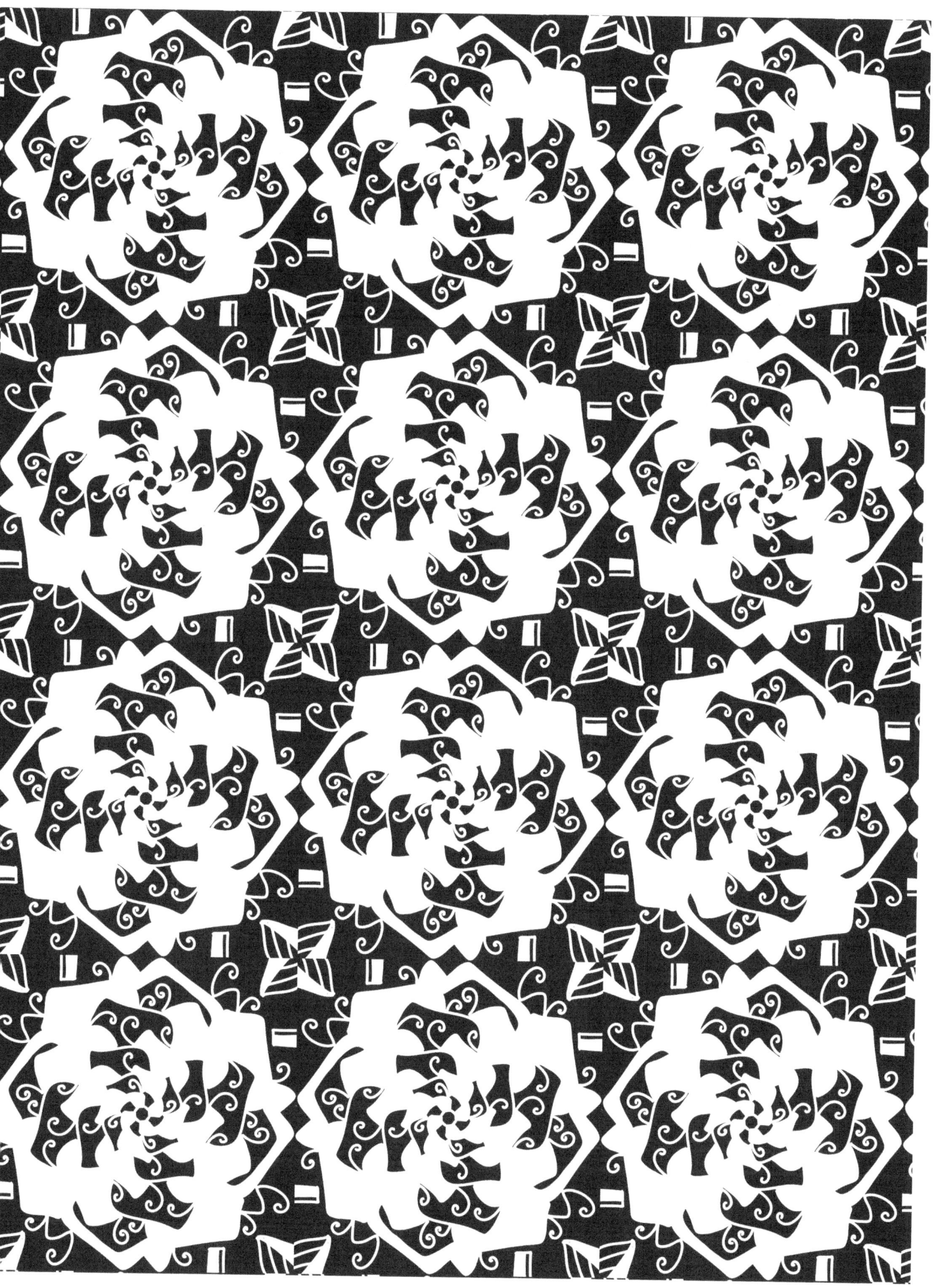

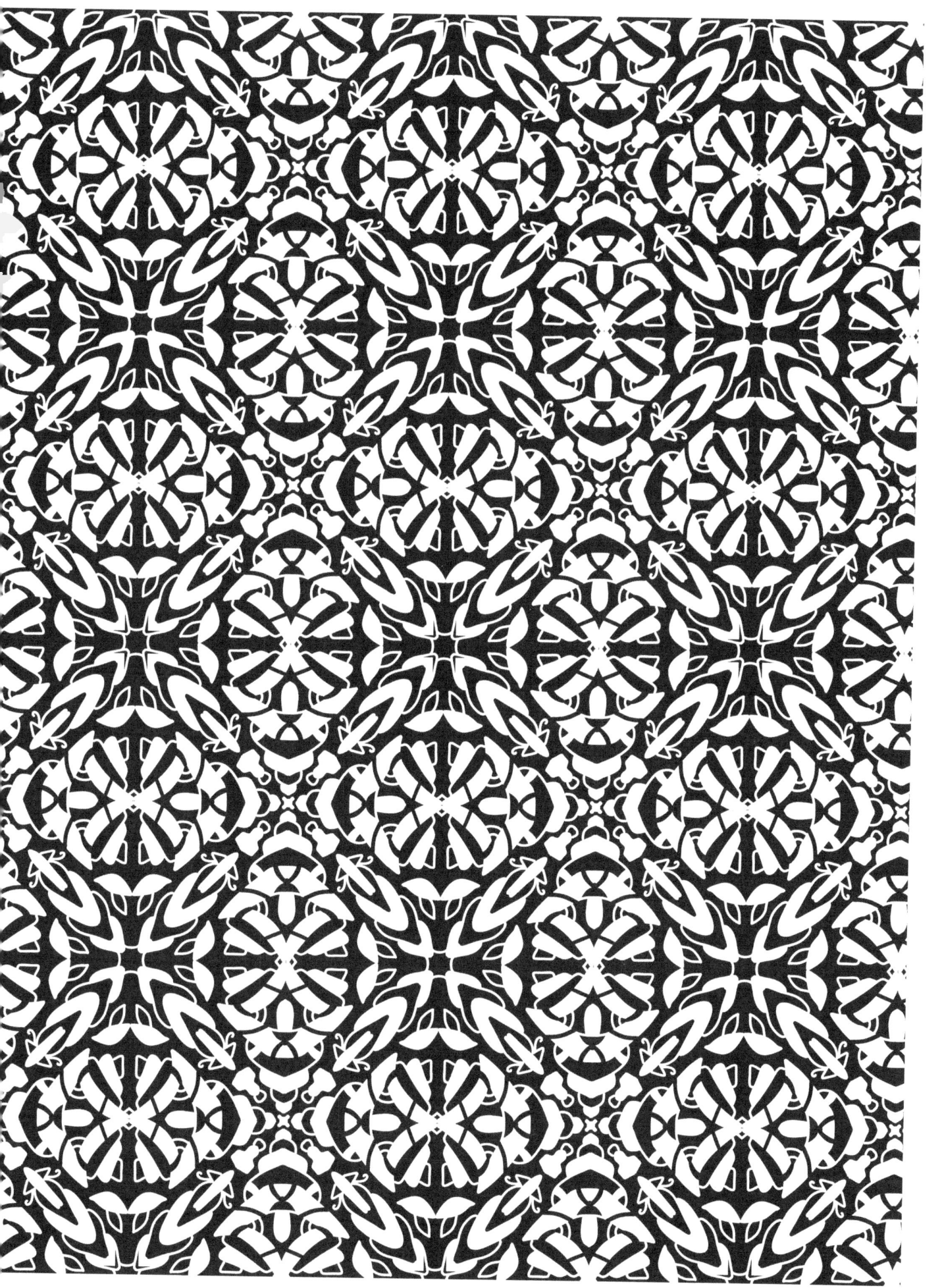

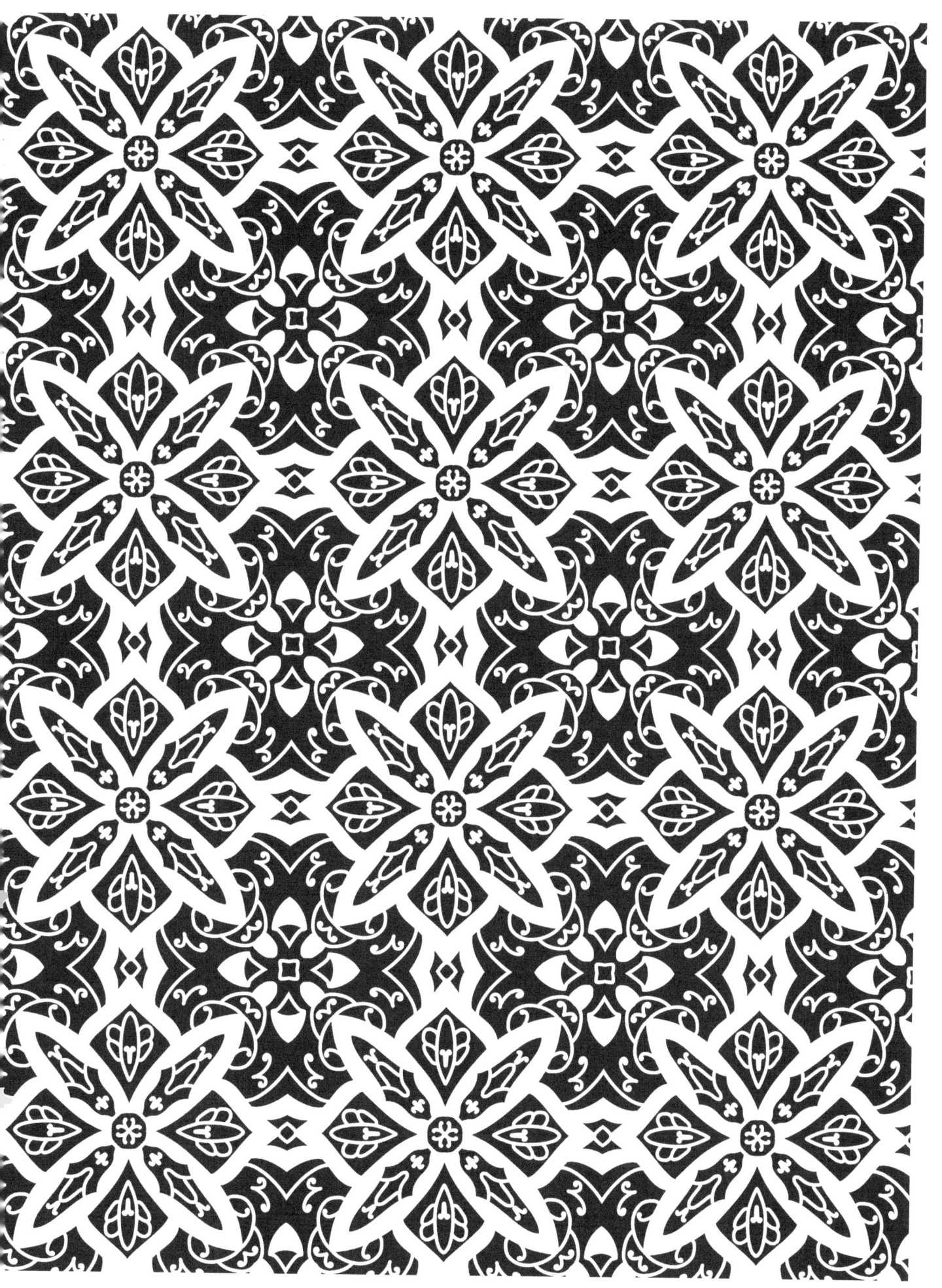

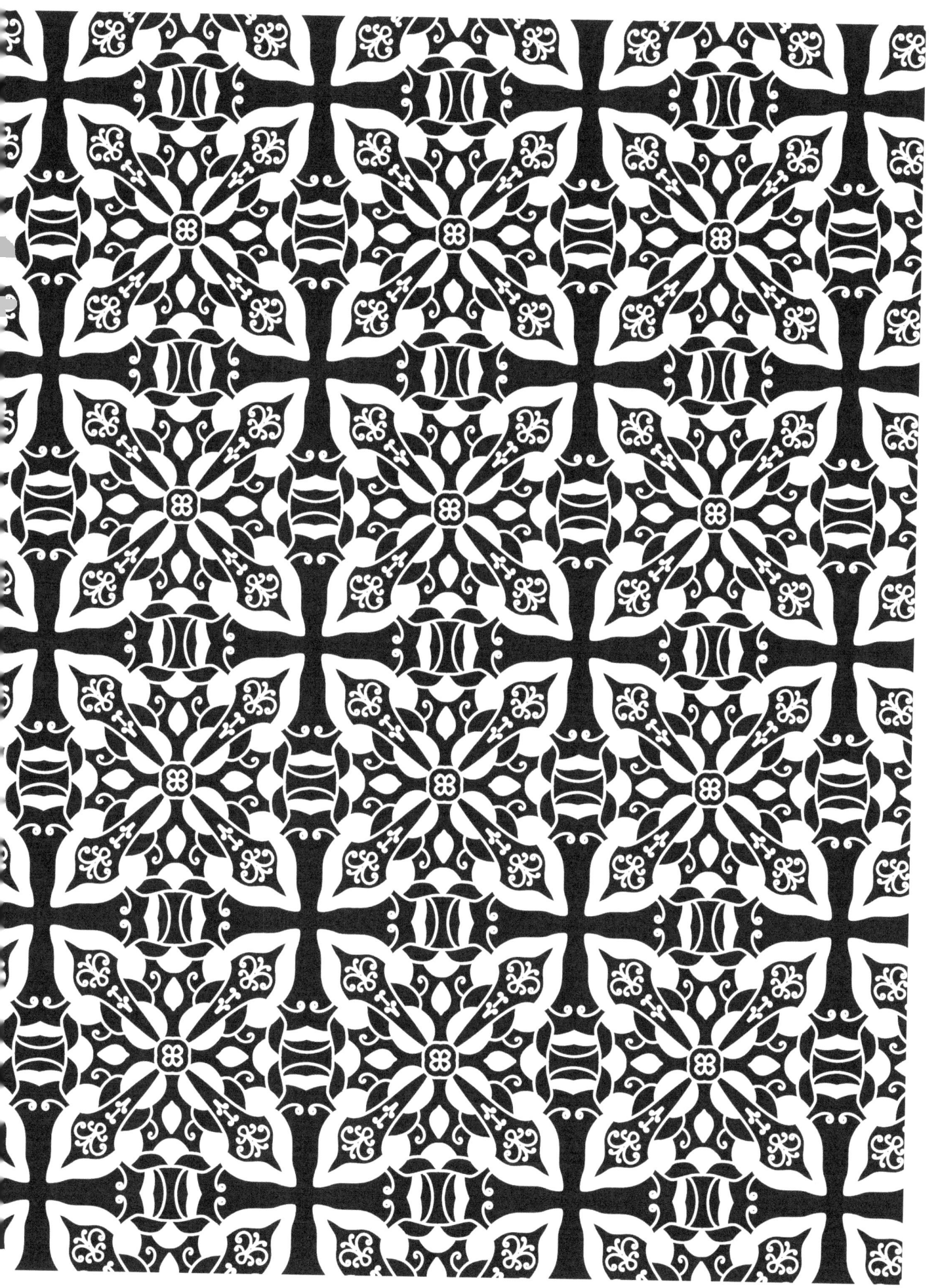

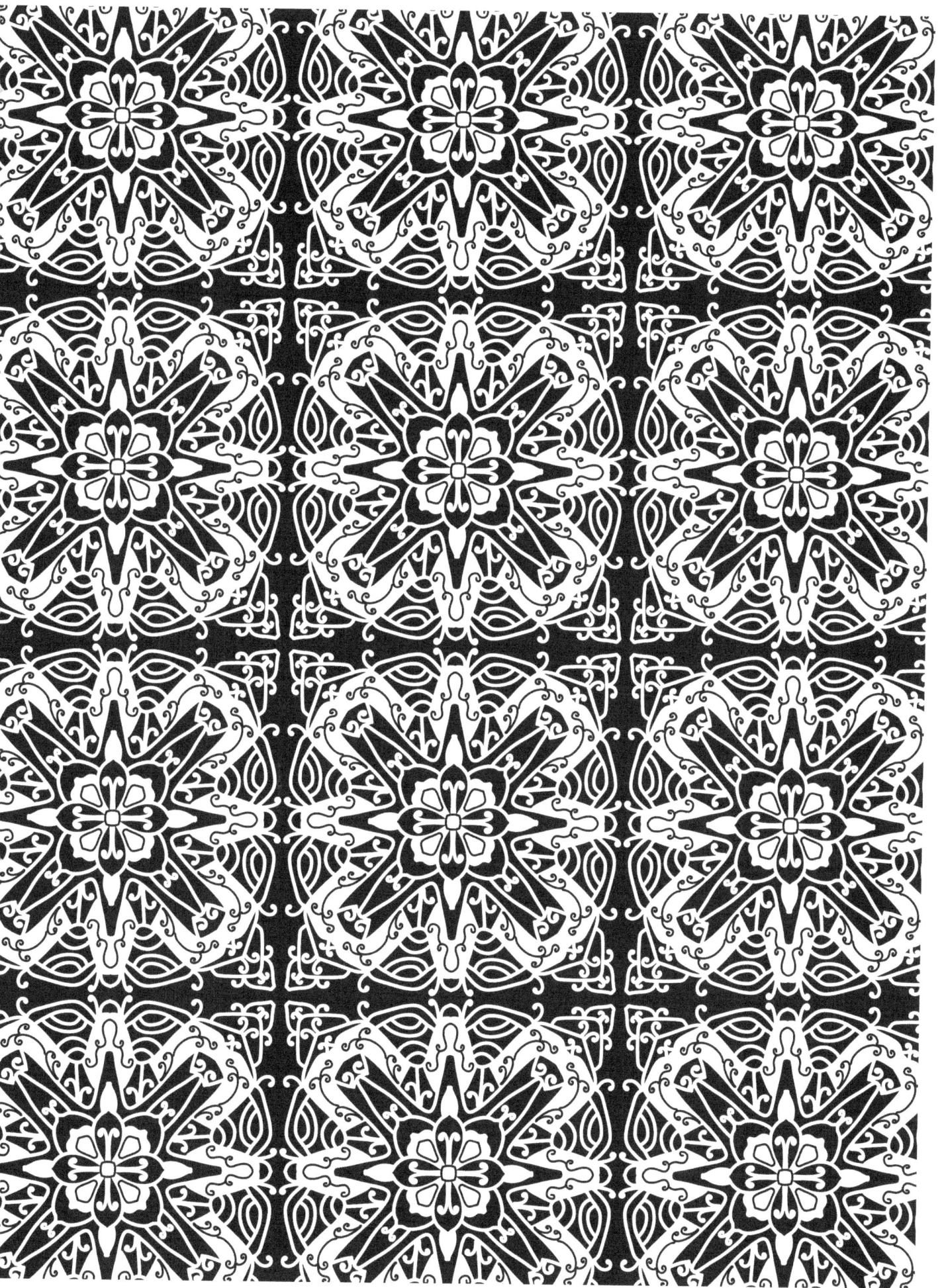

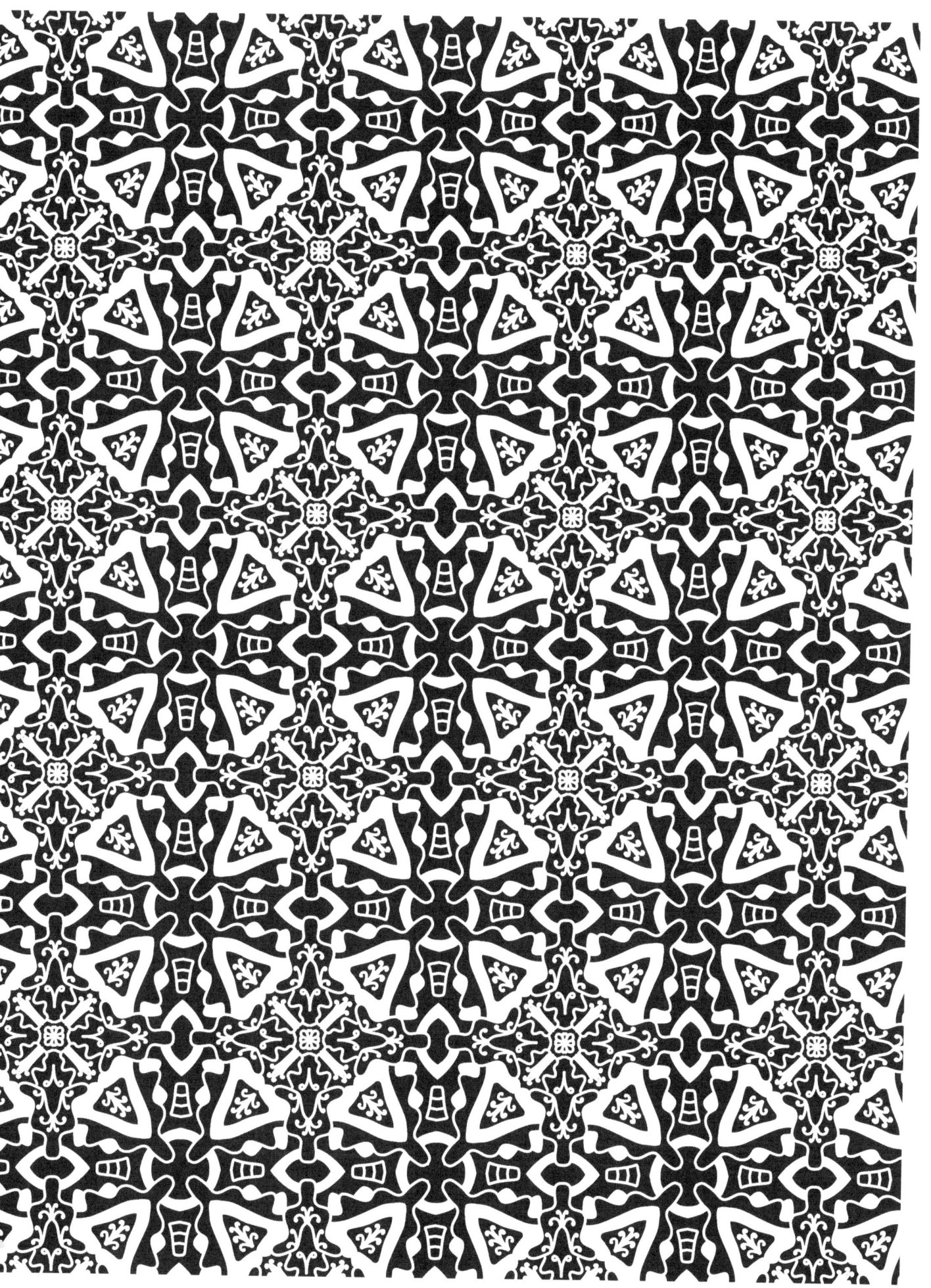

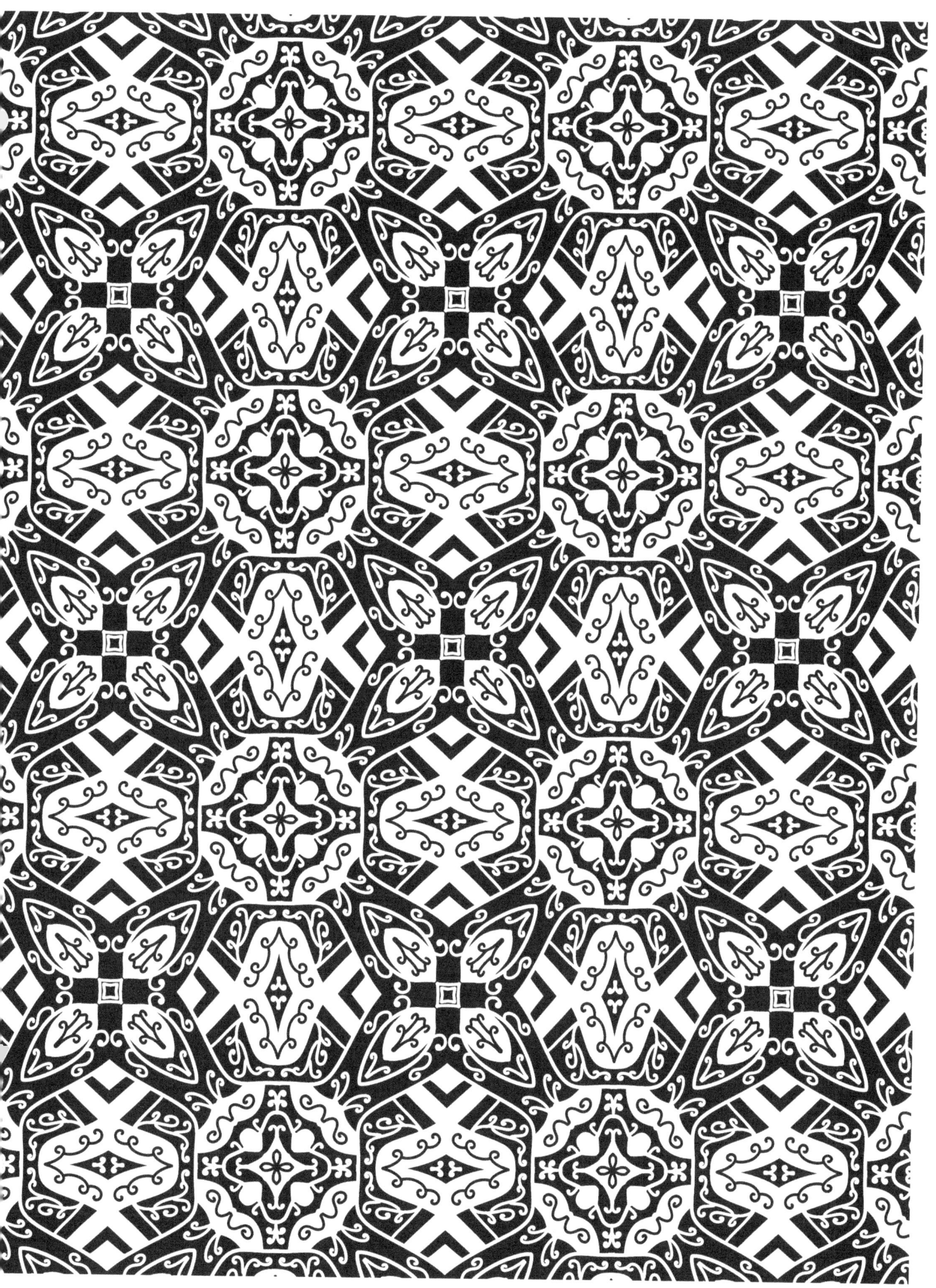

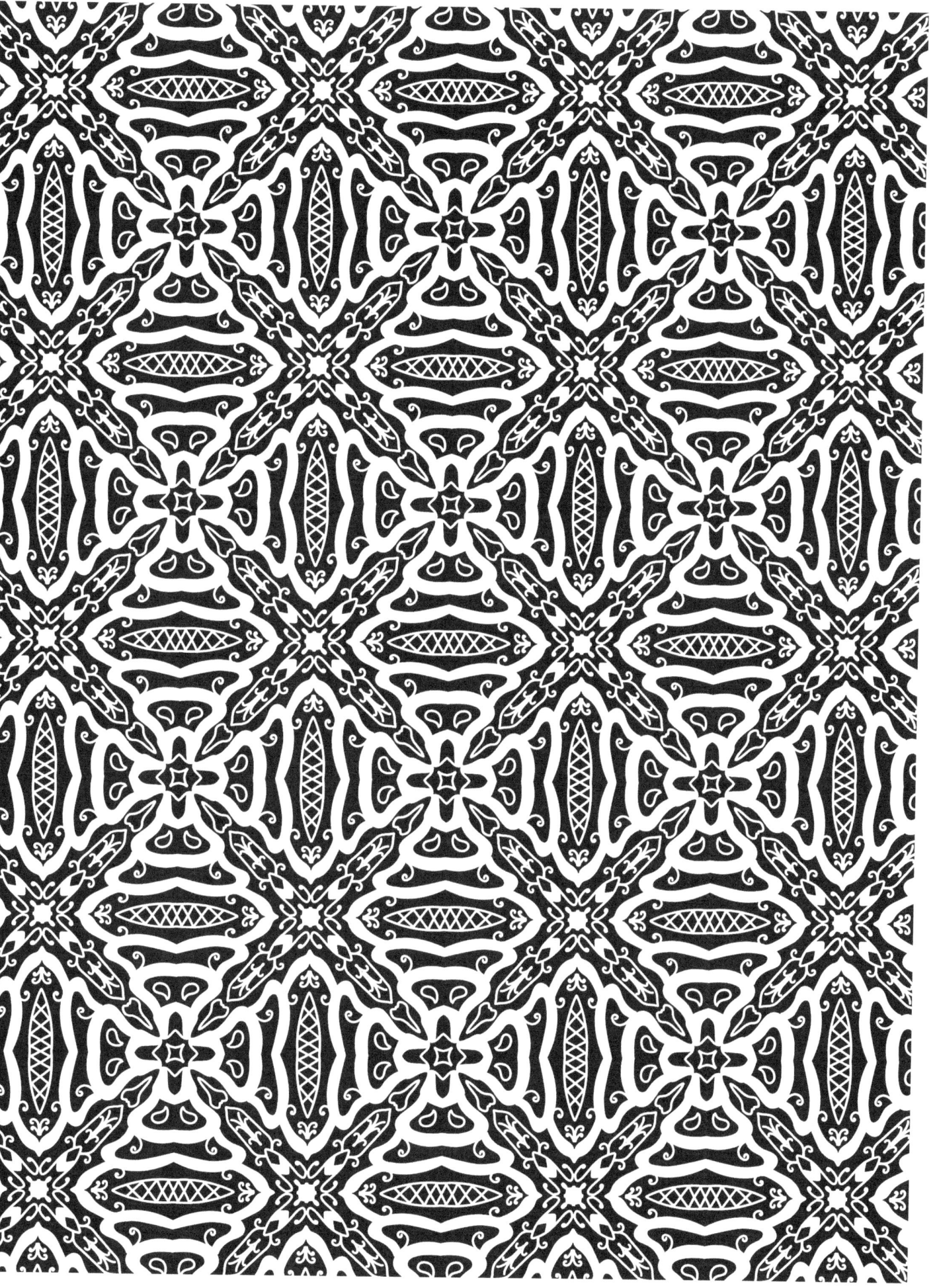

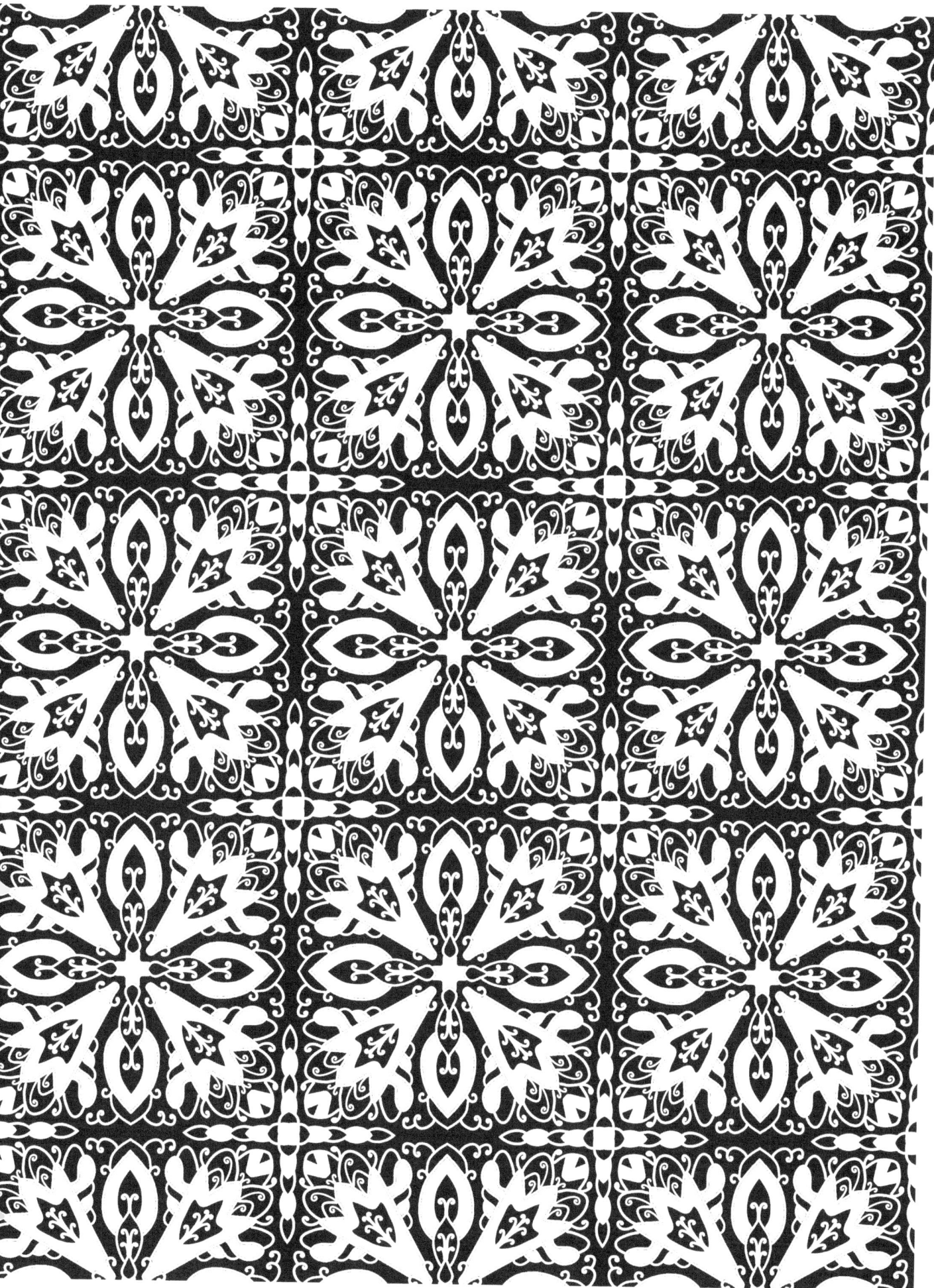

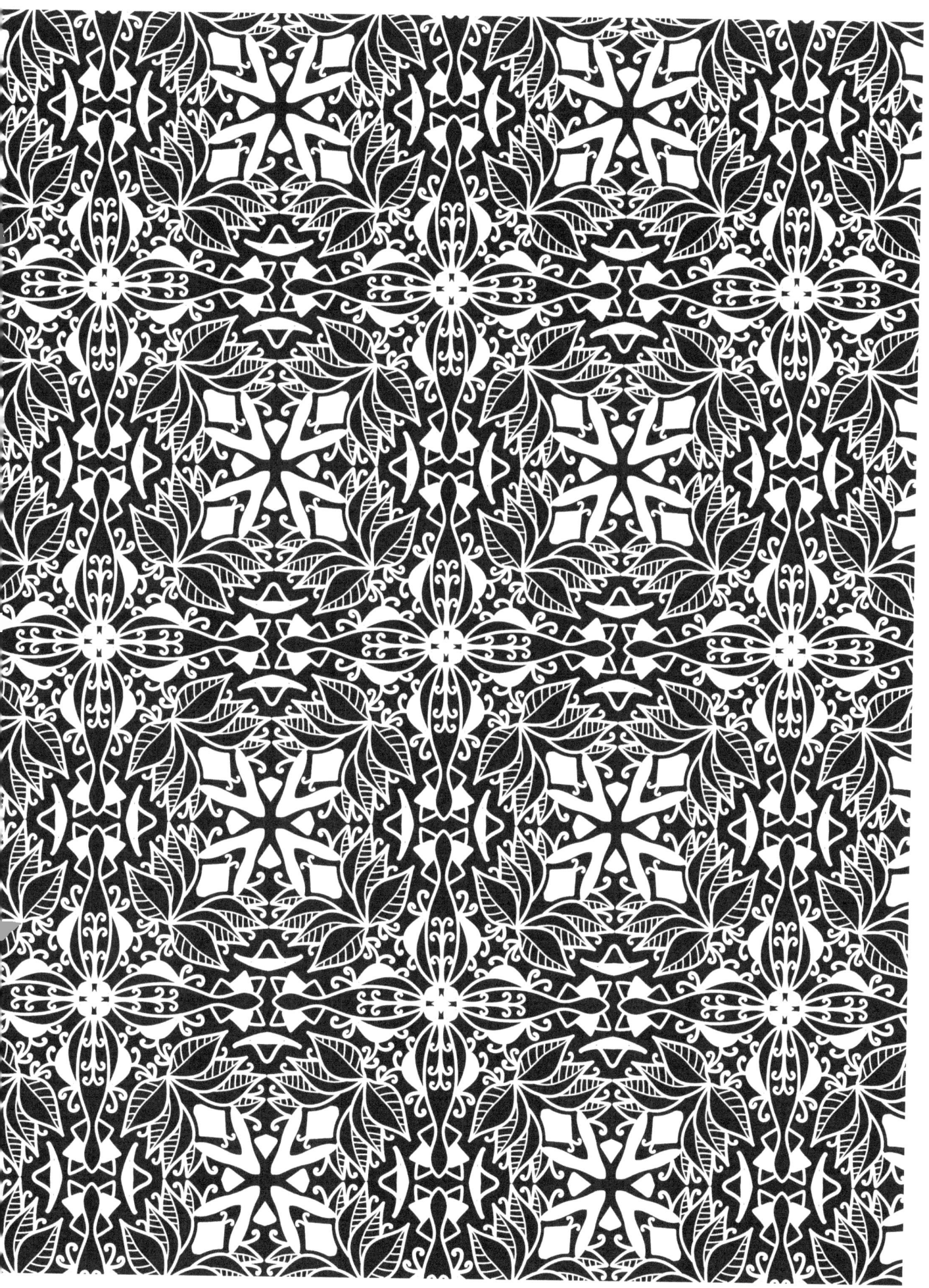

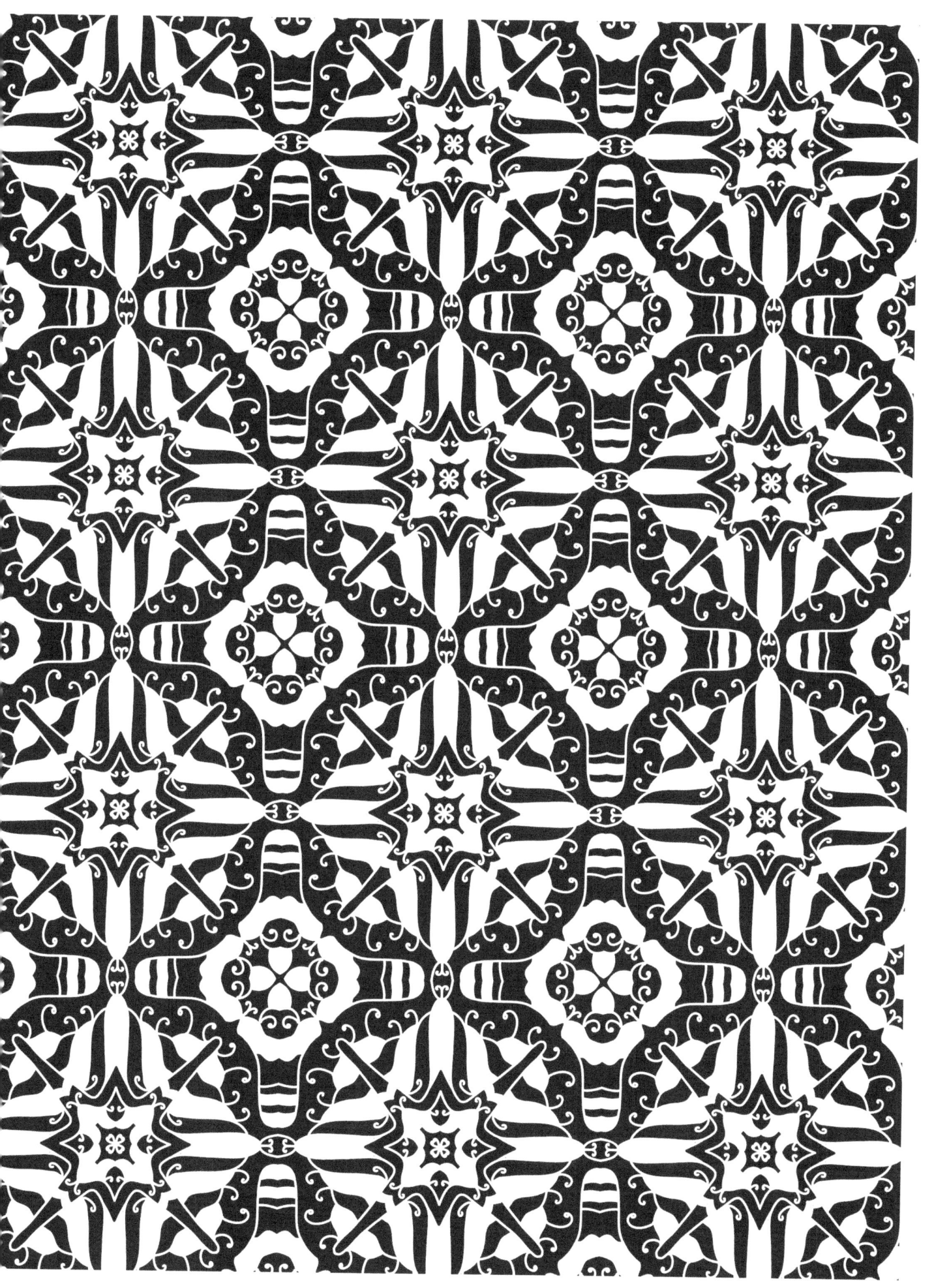

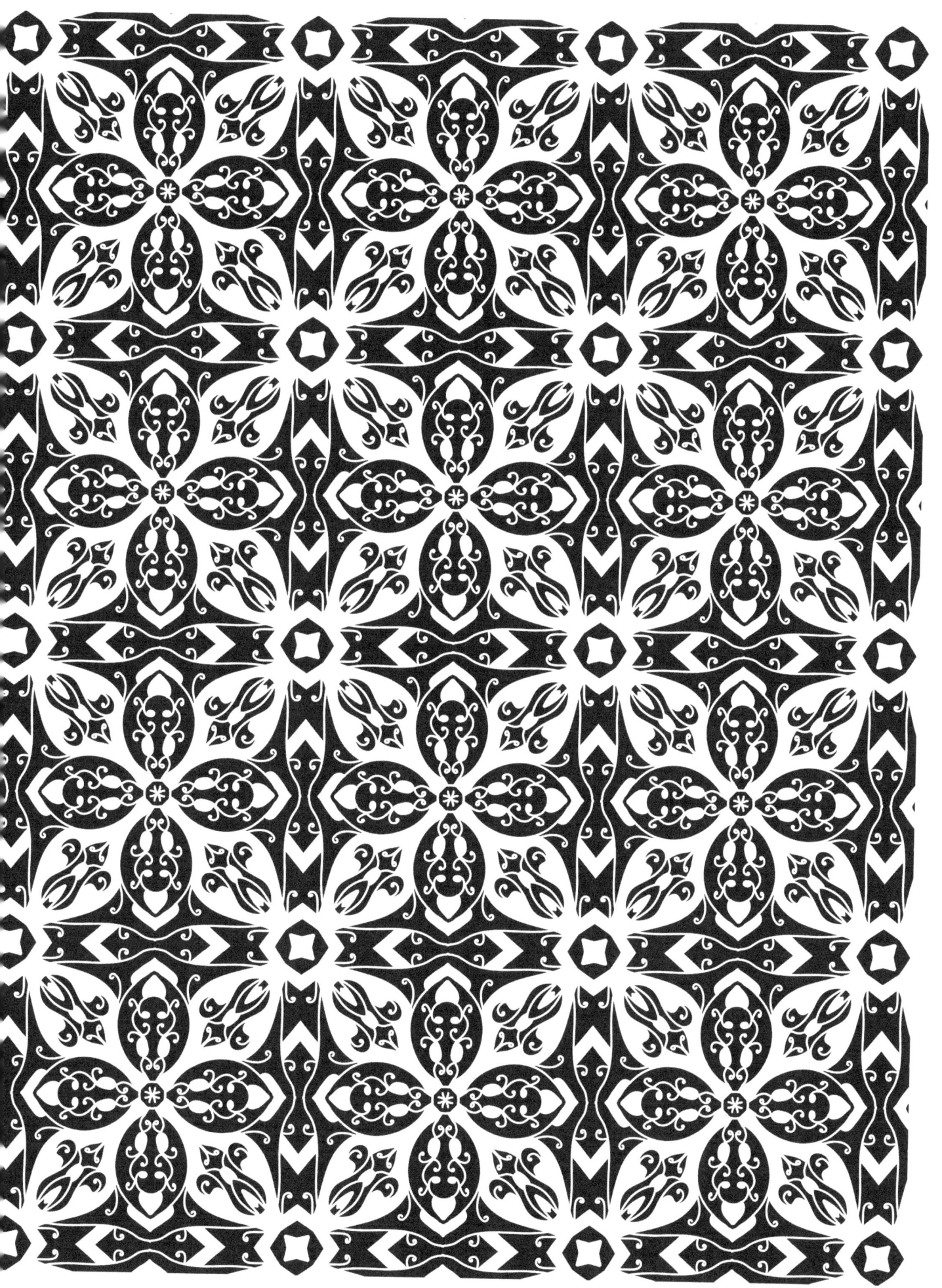

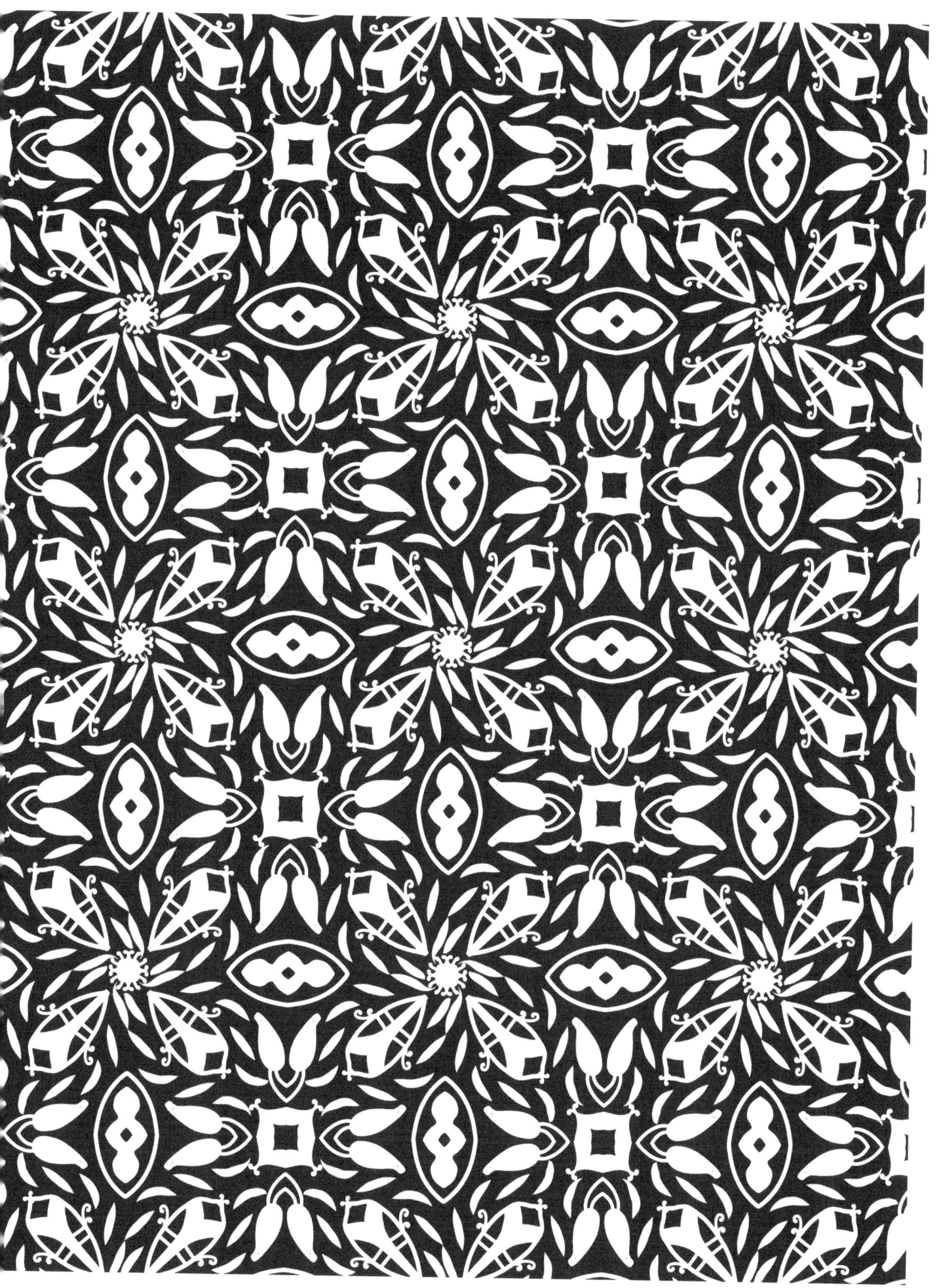

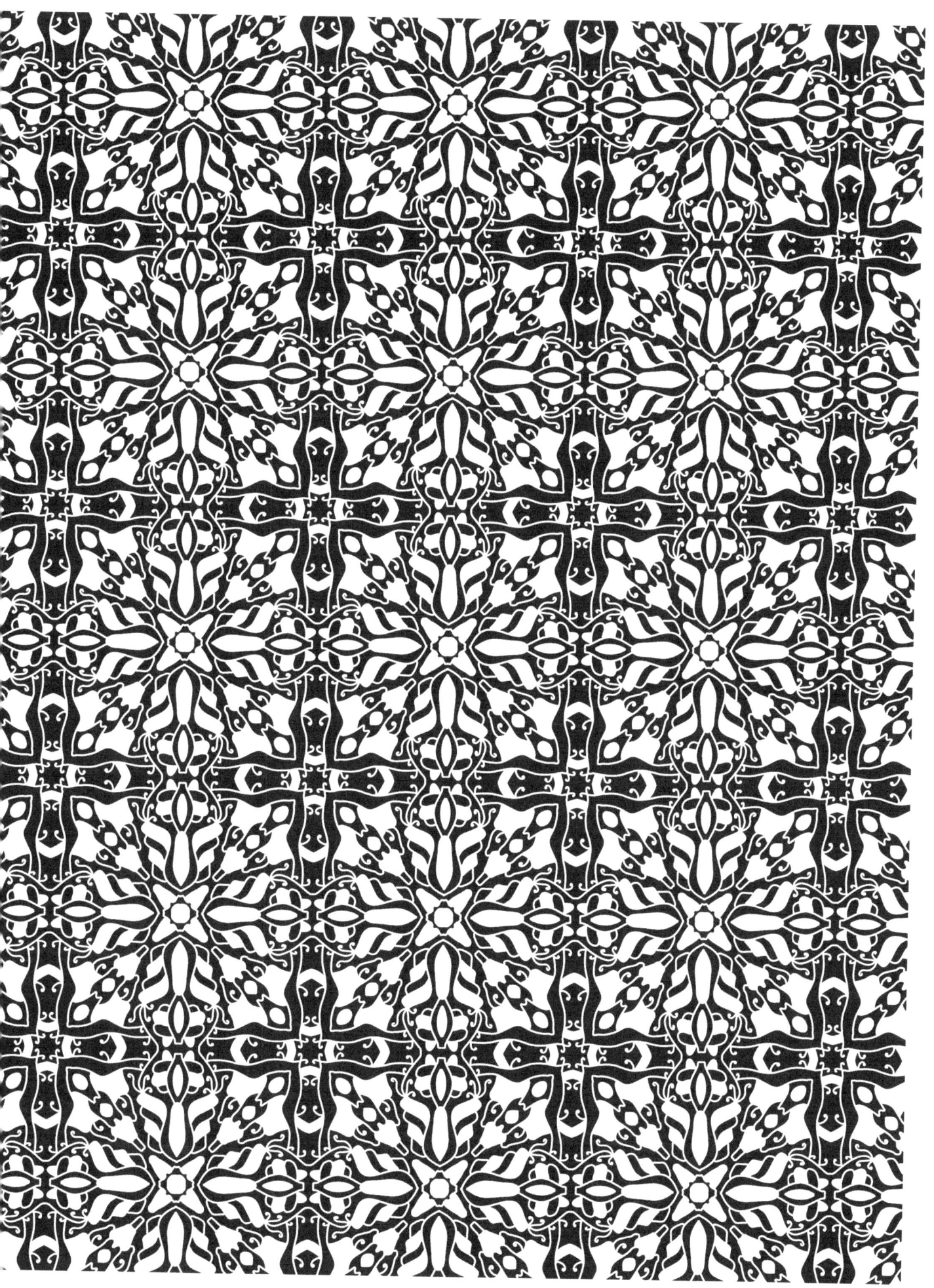

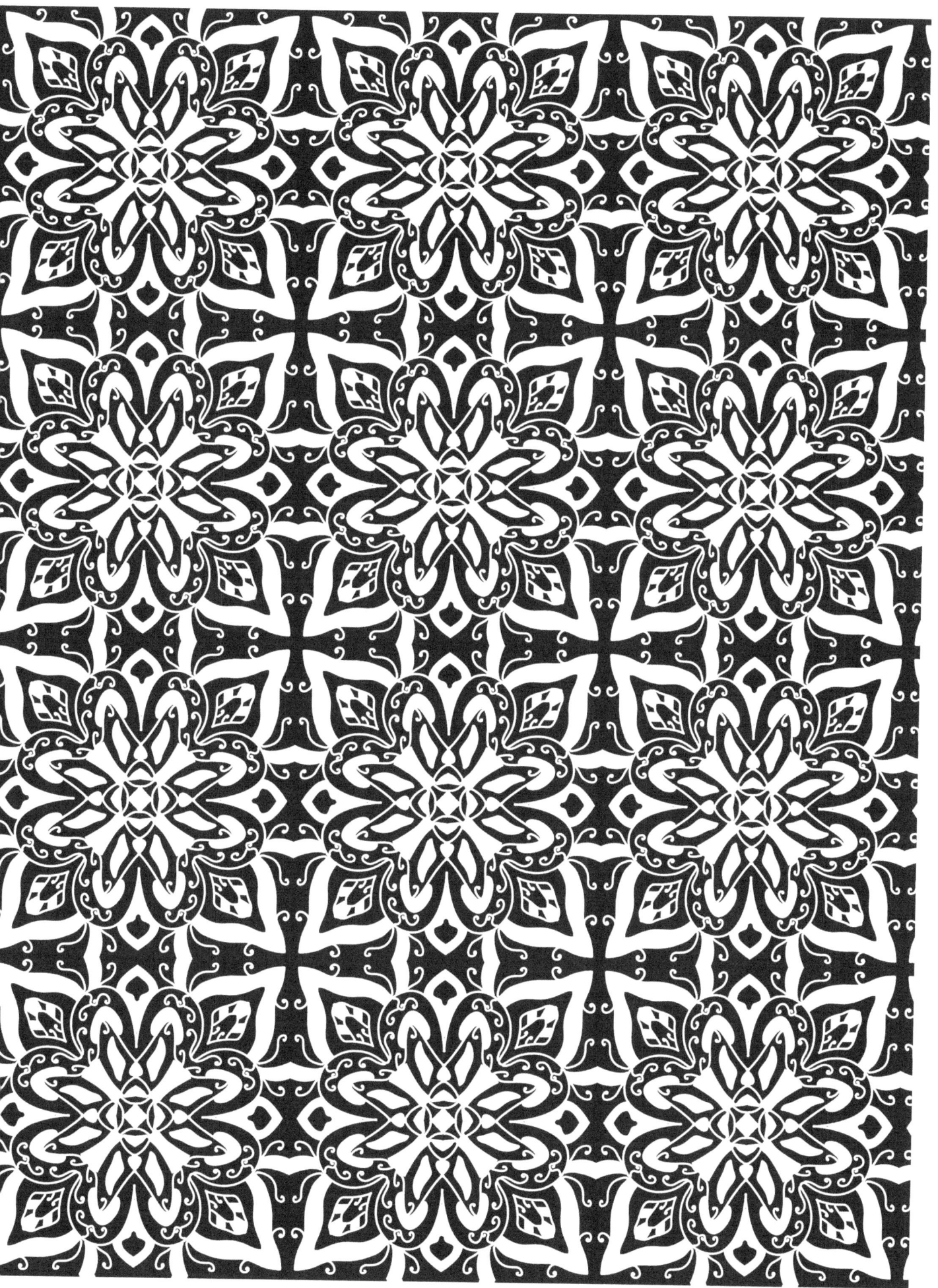

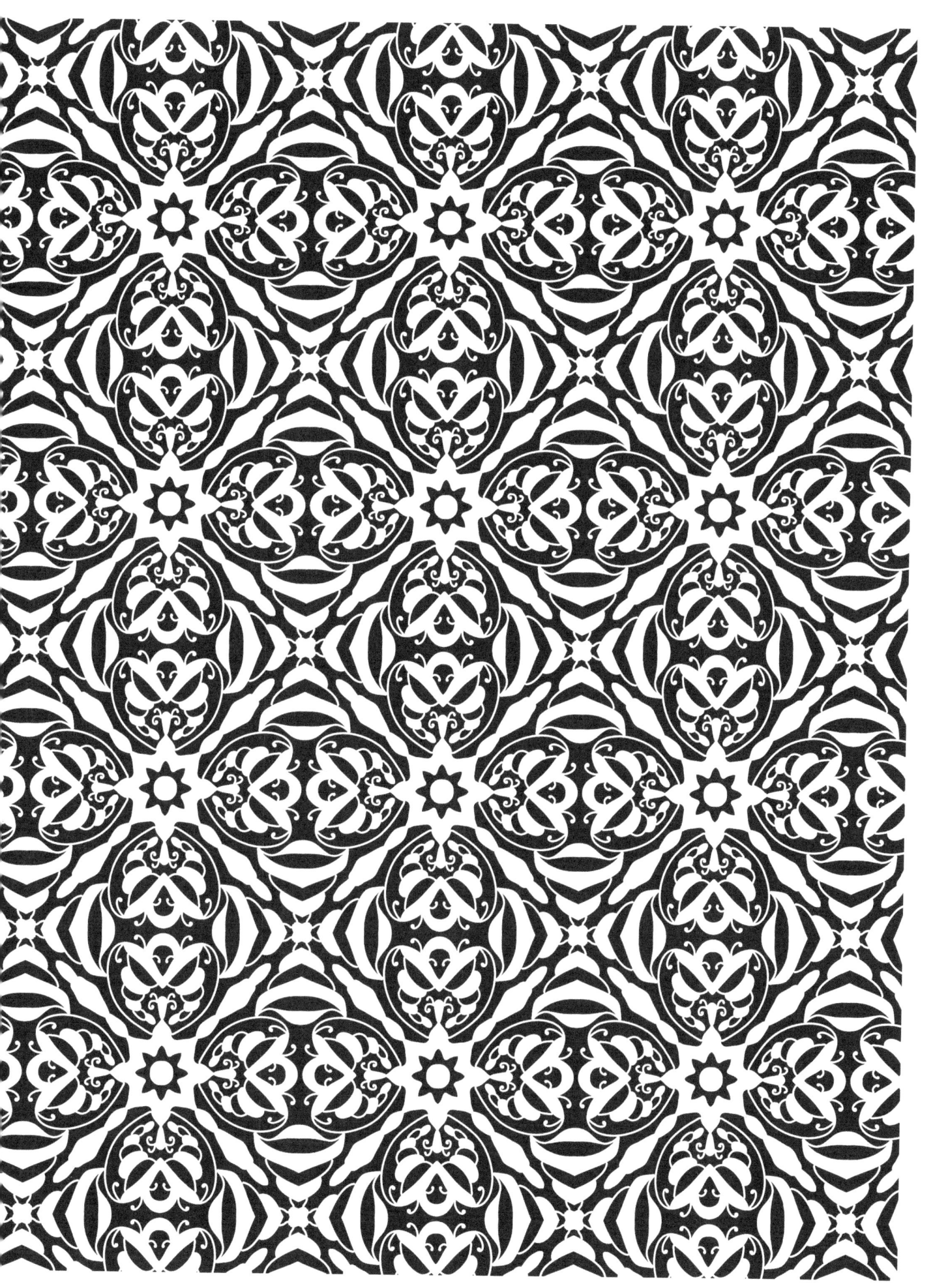

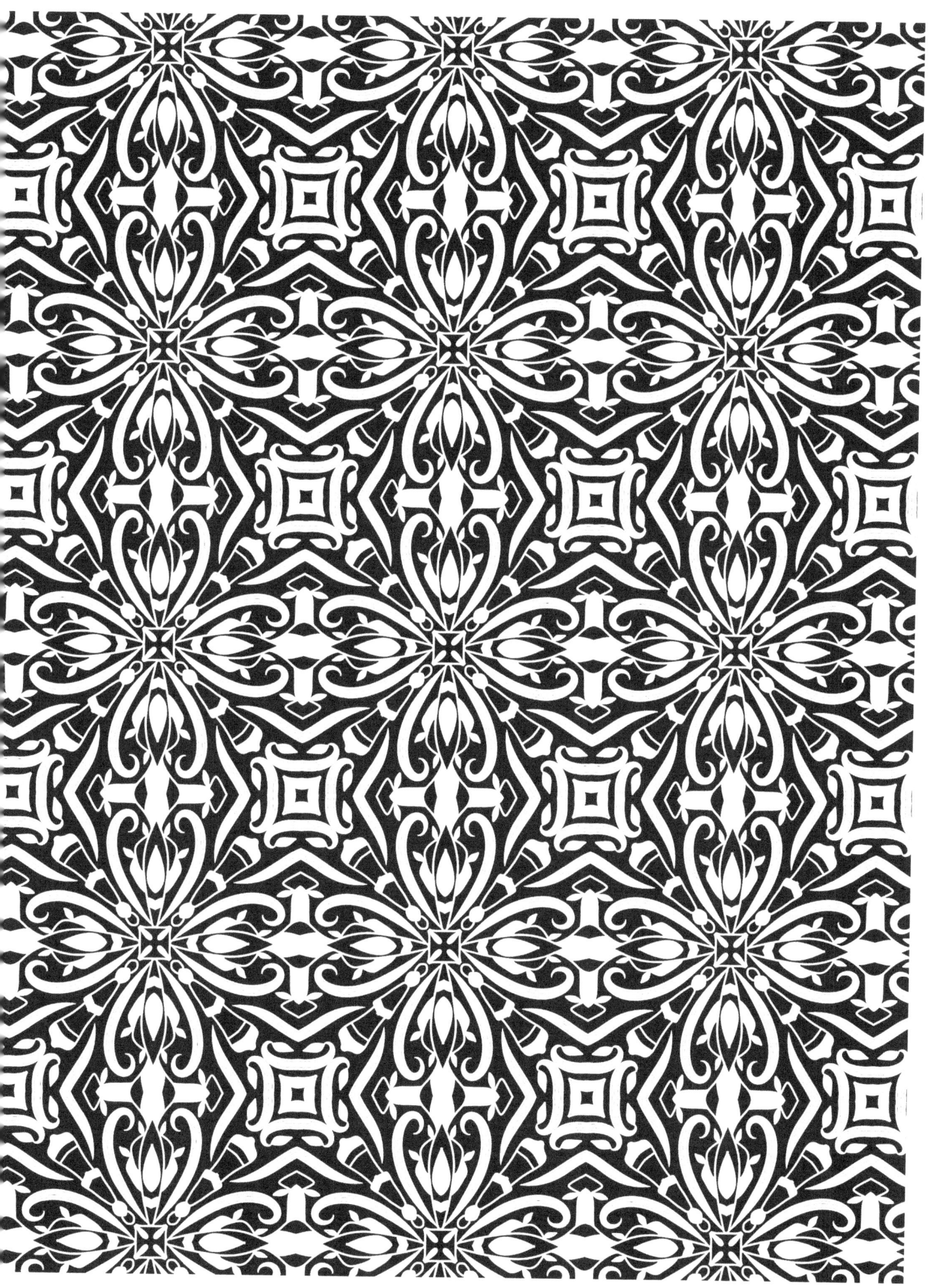

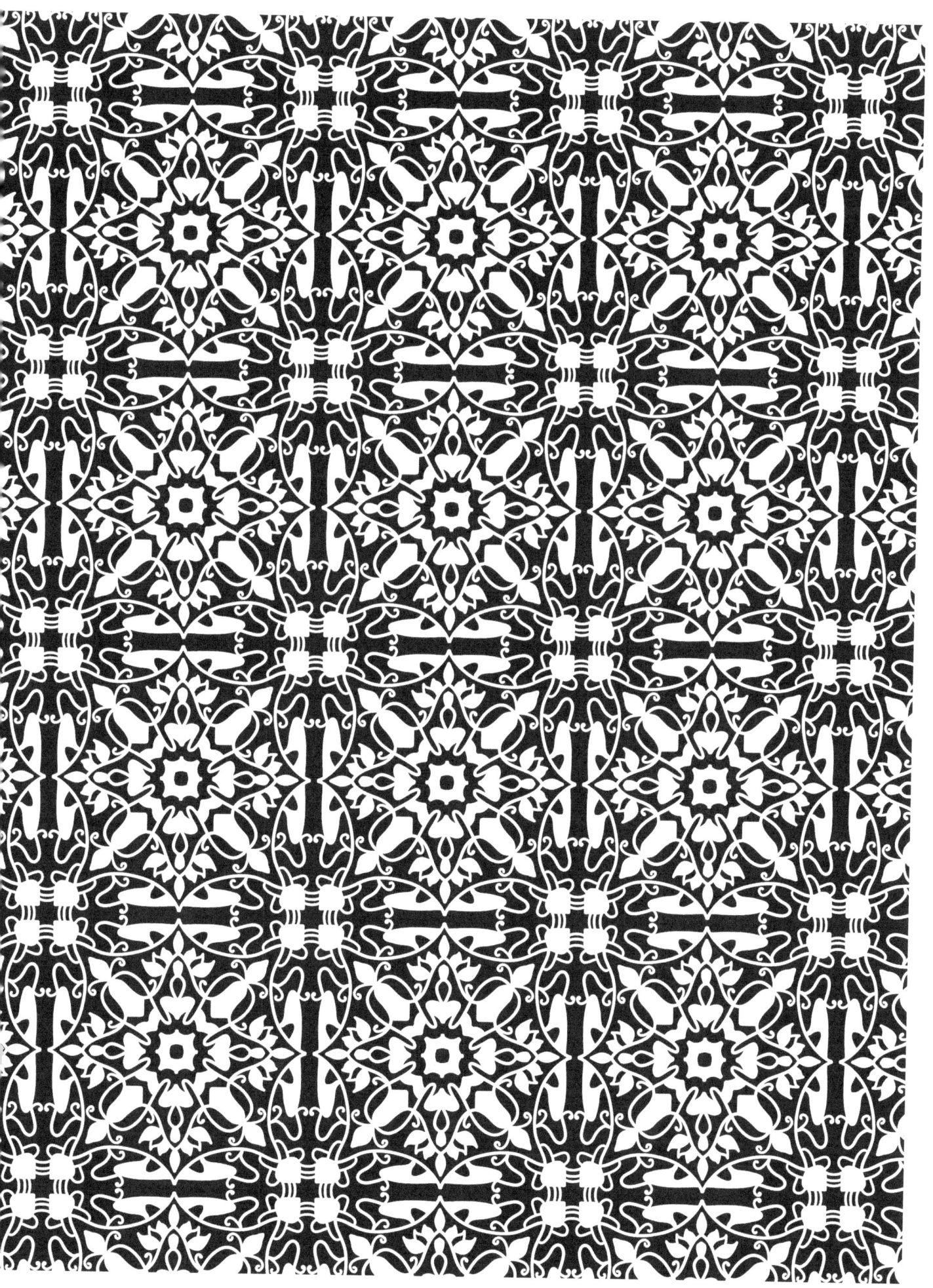

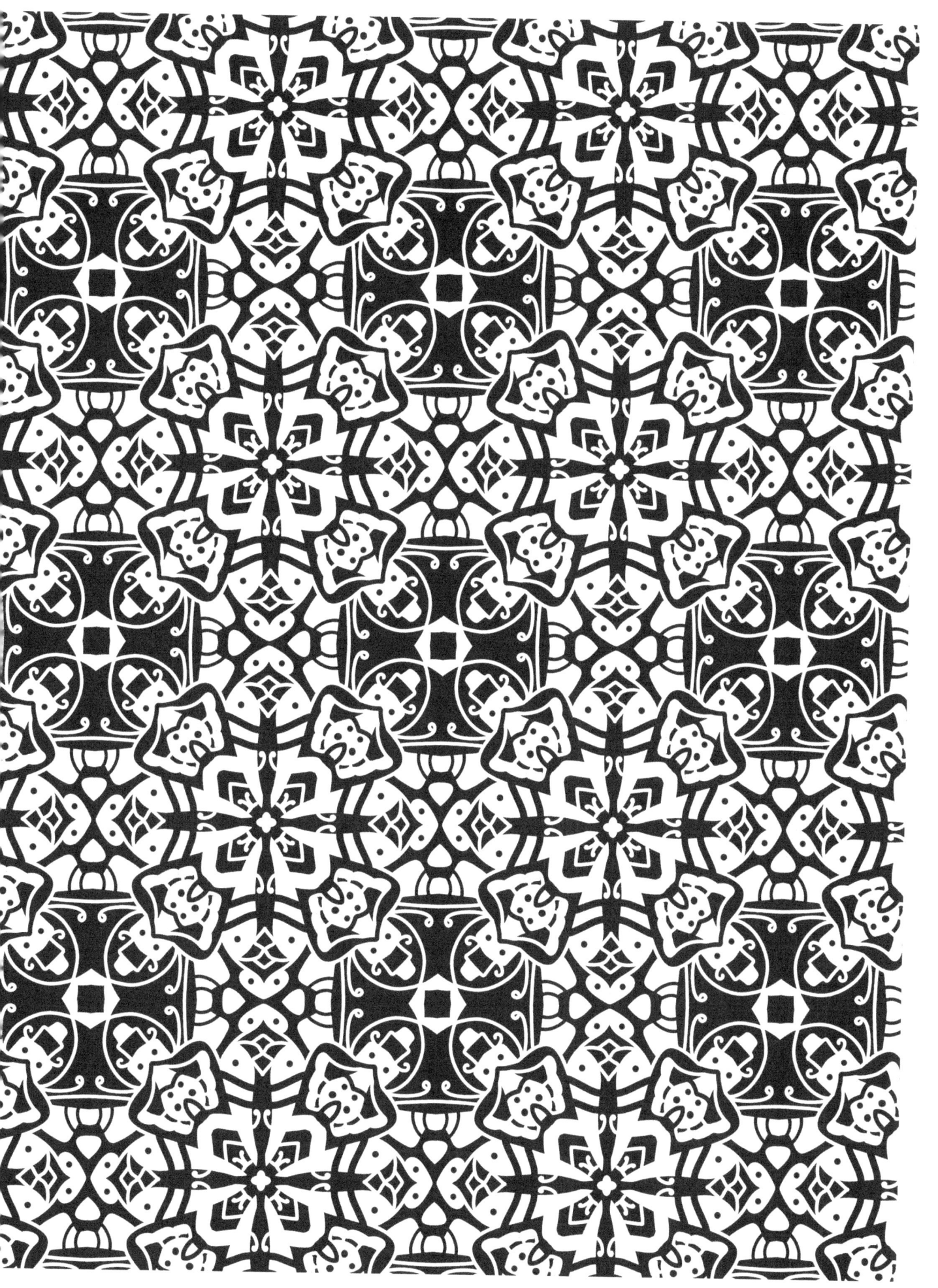

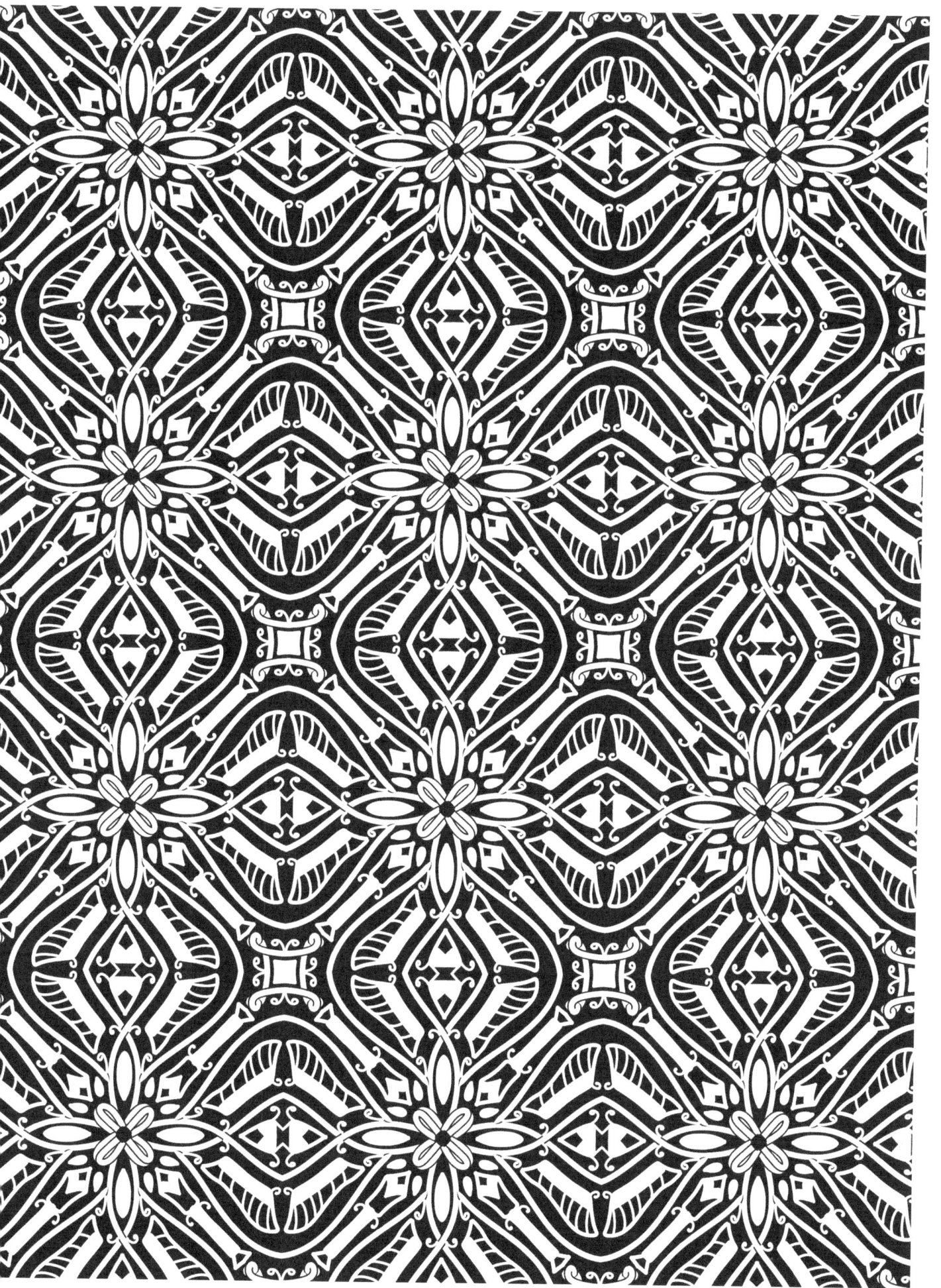

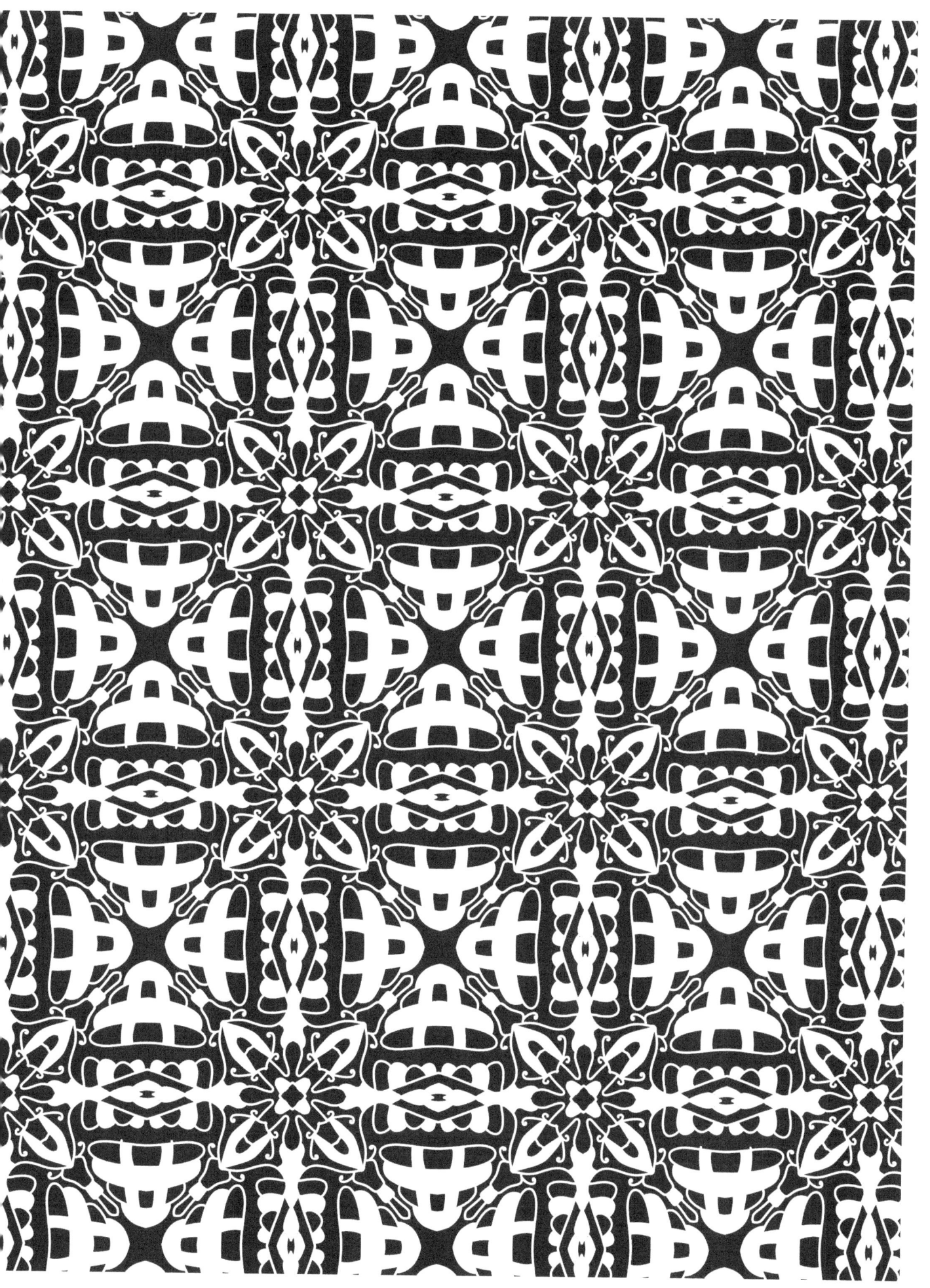

For more designs and upcoming books, please visit our facebook group at :

@coloringbooksandmandalas

http://www.asmazergui.com